IT IS AS EASY AS Z to A

A Journey Through the Alphabet

-Barbara W. McCoy, MS.-

wK Books

Dedication

*I must express my gratitude to
my 8th-grade teacher, Mrs. Teja, for believing in me
when I created the original version of this book
as a class project in 1998.
It took me over two decades, but
I followed her advice and published it.*

This is your invitation to come
alongside and explore the quest for
excellence as only a martial arts
athlete can.

Let it challenge you.

Let it encourage you.

Let it now begin.

Junbi

It is as Easy as Z to A:
A Journey Through the Alphabet

Zealous

The why, the inspiration behind the black belts' convincing powers of character. Being zealous is contagious and contributes to the existing knowledge of the art by sharing wisdom, values, and leadership. Z may commonly be known as the last letter of the alphabet. However, the alphabet begins with Z, a zealous spirit for a black belt.

YOU Matter. Martial arts exist because you are worth protecting. YOUR mind, YOUR body, and YOUR spirit are worth protecting. Be you and thrive. Be brave and change the world.

 Xenacious

Being diverse in capabilities, eager to learn new things, and willing to change and adapt due to their mental resilience. A trait of a black belt is creating space to experience and discover new possibilities and opportunities. A black belt is a world changer, training skills and living a life of passion despite the storms they may face.

Warrior

More than an adjective, the warrior is a noun for the athlete facing their fears, getting back up, and fiercely walking bravely into the light. A warrior is more than a fighter. Individuals identifying as warriors regulate their mental, physical, and emotional components to seize the moment with the correct response over a flustered reaction.

Victorious

A black belt faces each moment, tiny or enormous, ready to celebrate the things that made them smile, fight for those who cannot, and do the next right thing. Confronting adversity with a steadfast, able, mighty, and resilient heart. Emerging from the setbacks covered by a cloud of humility.

Unforgettable

A strong influence that is memorable is what makes a black belt exceptional. The moments of their performances and mannerisms intentionally show habits of sportsmanlike behavior. Becoming a black belt is not something that happens overnight. It is a journey, a lifestyle that one cannot simply forget.

Thankfulness

By showing thankfulness, the black belt treats their body with respect and kindness, pushing it to new levels of excellence each day. Showing appreciation with a constant attitude of gratitude allows one to have the spirit of thankfulness guiding one's steps. In all aspects of black belts' lives, in word and deed, there is an air of humility rather than expectancy.

Sportsmanship

The ability to encourage others despite facing disappointment after a competitive situation. Sportsmanship is a fundamental priority for a black belt to keep things fun and provide a structure that empowers the sports legacy. Maintaining a good attitude and persevering rather than cutting down our opponents or teammates is the choice one faces after being acknowledged victorious.

Respect

A humble attitude to self, individuals, and
facilities where individuals leave things
better than when they arrive. For a black belt, the
factors of respect start with controlling emotions
and choosing against bullying or destroying things.
The application of respect is to know when and how
to use one's skill to protect themselves in all senses
of one's mind, body, and spirit.

Quotable

Quotable with the power of words speaking life, like pictures and posters with quotes bringing life into the room, are the black belt leaders. The black belt, internally and externally, speaks powerful quotes to overcome adversity, reads for inspiration, and, in those quotable moments, often is slower and quieter with their actions.

Power

The definition of power as a verb and noun acknowledges what one must do, having and knowing the provision of giving and receiving. Using the word power to define one's capabilities allows the possibility of an external influence to occur. For a black belt, this concept shapes us and represents one's character as it is displayed in these moments that require a choice that often challenges the standard.

Obedience

Obedience aligns with joy, doing the right thing because it is correct, and seeing gratitude from those intentional steps. One faithful step after another, saying yes not out of guilt but from self-respect and respect for the individuals in your community. Even when the black belt does not understand, they say, "Yes, Sir," and do the next right thing.

oble

The word noble is often in the context of other words like true, pure, proper, lovely, and admirable. For black belts, the word noble can be a characteristic of who they are and their actions. To them, being noble is to make their own decisions with integrity, courage, and kindness to overcome the negativity in their lives and world.

Motivation

What is behind your actions? What are those thoughts? The narrative that you tell yourself? For a black belt, inner dialogue is robust and catalyzes their behavior. That is where their desire, their intrinsic motivation, is found.

Loyalty

To self, to others, to your art …
Loyalty is an adjective that could be empowering
or used as a form of control. For a black belt, loyalty
is incorporated in the complex and
tenacious willingness to serve, not having to agree
on everything. It is an expression of honor and is
never asked for.

Kindness

Kindness is an action of any size that shows excellent strength when activated in moments united with creativity, love, and beauty. It brings an abundance of peace as the black belt fills another's cup with a gentleness that gives strength to transform the situation.

oy

Regardless of the outward experience, the ability to regulate the internal circumstance is the feeling of great pleasure and satisfaction when training for yourself. That is what joy is: not letting comparison steal the feeling of possibility when the moment does not feel fun and training anyway.

Indomitable Spirit

Indomitable Spirit is that internal drive to overcome the present darkness for that optimal performance that reminds the black belt of their identity. A spirit of hope that, instead of pressure, cultivates friendship and partnerships and strengthens confidence in their next step.

umility

This compassion, patience, and diligent gentleness that defines the core of humility shows humanity's depth. Showing humility alongside tenacity, vision, passion, and authenticity makes a black belt.

Greatness

Greatness, as defined by a black belt, is more than a term of power. It is defined by the actions taken toward the life they want. Along with success, one is made great by failures, for persistence takes you to the next level.

Focus

The narrative of the black belt mindset can pause in the present moment, calming their mind to create a space of precise and controlled thinking. Remaining focused on the finish line first, not perfection, while helping others on the team to do the same, moving forward through strategies, progress, and consistent effort.

Excellence

Making measurable leaps and bounds in one's strength, self-control, and personal development in relationships. A Black Belt commits to the connection between passion and skill in all they do.

Development

Managing one's energy properly and learning to manage emotions takes an active and intentional commitment. The story of a black belt comes with the exhorting, encouraging, and imploring of an agent of change who questions, reframes problems, and repeatedly demonstrates the desired behavior.

Character

There is a difference between experiencing a
failure and being one. You are the same person
before and after a loss. The strength of
character enables the black belt to
get up and keep moving when setbacks occur.

# Behavior

Training like a black belt is active, not passive. It involves verbal instruction and modeling desired behaviors and character traits.

Attitude

Being black belt tough is an attitude that allows you to rise above mental and physical obstacles that might cause others to give up!

Every journey has a starting point; not all journeys are equal in their expectations and intensity.

As you embark on your journey as a martial arts athlete, remember that it is entirely your path to follow.

Enjoy it.
Embrace it.

Although it may be difficult, the result is valuable.

You are worth it.

Baro.

Author's Note: Thank you for reading this improved version of a class assignment from 1998 that inspired an Instagram series for McCoy's Action Karate in 2023.

AVAILABLE FROM WHISTLEKICK BOOKS PUBLISHING

BY JEREMY LESNIAK

Non-Fiction

The Martial Artist's Handbook

12 Months to Health

How Not to Hold a Tournament

Stronger people Are Harder to Kill

Press Release Mastery

Simpler Social Media

Starting to Sell on Amazon

Fiction

Faith: The Katana Chronicles - Book One

The Katana Chronicles - Book Two **COMING SOON!**

BY JENNI SIU

The Origin of Master Hopkick: Beginnings

The Origin of Master Hopkick: Beginnings - Special Edition

The Origin of Master Hopkick: Beginnings - Instructor's Edition (w/ Chris Rickard)

The Origin of Master Hopkick: Lessons

The Origin of Master Hopkick Book Three **COMING SOON!**

BY CHRIS RICKARD

The Instructor's Guide to Jenni Siu's The Origin of Master Hopkick: Beginnings - Mat Chat and Classroom Discussion Guide

BY JENNI NATHER

Modern Moms of Martial Arts: Volume One

BY BARBARA W. MCCOY, MS

It's as Easy as Z to A: A Journey Through the Alphabet

INSPIRED BY WHISTLEKICK MARTIAL ARTS RADIO

Collections

Celebrating Women in the Martial Arts
Legends of the Martial Arts
What Advice Would You Give Martial Artists 100 Years From Now?
A Journey Into the Badlands w/ Daniel Wu, Emily Beecham, and Sherman Augustus
The Karate Kid & Cobra Kai Collection
Restomp The Interviews w/ Master ken, Matt page, and Joseph Conway

One-on-One Interviews

Tony Blauer
Mr. Don "The Dragon" Wilson
Shihan Bas Rutten
Bill "superfoot" Wallace
Adrian Paul
Sensei Fumio Demura
Iain Abernethy
Five Faces of Kempo
Jhoon Rhee
Stephen Hayes
Nathan Porter

SEARCH US ON AMAZON FOR MORE TITLES!

wK Books

We Want to Hear from You!

Reviews are an important part of how others find our books, and they help us create content you love. If you enjoyed this book, please visit the associated Amazon product listing and leave us a review. We will use your feedback to help create more content catered towards you, our loyal readers.

Thank you!!

DON'T MISS OUR EVENTS!

ALL-IN WEEKEND

This 2-day martial arts event will be half training experience and half retreat. The cost of the event includes all of your training, your lodging, food, and an event shirt. All you have to do is show up, and we'll take care of the rest.

FREE TRAINING DAY

whistlekick's Free Training Day is exactly what the name says - one day of the year where martial artists come together to share and learn, all for free. There is no admission fee at this event, instructors are not paid, and whistlekick picks up the tab for the venue and any other logistical costs.

MARTIAL SUMMIT

Martial Summit is our vision for the future. A place where martial artists, from all over the world, of all systems and styles, come together to share. This 4-day event includes Free Training Day Northeast as well as the Never Settle Awards Banquet.

Follow the QR codes above or visit whistlekick.com and click on "For Individuals" to find all the latest info on our incredible events!

12 Months to Health

By Jeremy Lesniak

This book is designed to help you establish and reinforce 12 simple, inexpensive habits to achieve a healthier you in 12 months.

Available on Amazon!

"Mr. Lesniak has laid out a well-researched, simple, and gradual guide to real success in incorporating healthy habits into one's daily life. I look forward to sharing this with my patients as a partner in their journey toward better health."
— Joshua Singer, Licensed Acupuncturist at River Street Wellness, Montpelier, Vermont

"Setting just the right goal is hard to do, and starting with consistent, bite-sized, achievable goals is the way to achieve real change in your health."
— Irvin Eisenberg, Masters in Occupational Therapy, Structural Integrator and Owner of Resilience Occupational Therapy

"Our healthcare system, as it is built, right now, is largely not designed to help you until AFTER chronic disease strikes. Even preventative health endorsed by your doctor is left to the small choices you make daily, by yourself, well outside of the walls of the clinic."
— Joshua T. White, MD, MBA, Chief Medical Officer, Gifford Medical Center

"12 things that ANYONE can do that will make a vast difference to their life."
— Daniel Eagles

"A single focus for a month makes it much more likely that I will be able to make sustainable changes."
— StaciAnne KaeLeigh Grove

FREE whistlekick Flexibility Program!

Yes, I said FREE! This program is designed by and for martial artists with features you won't find in any other program, at any price. The Flexibility Program is rooted in the latest science, immensely effective, and different from what most of us were taught.

The FREE whistlekick 30-Day Challenge

The program is a FREE and COMPLETE standalone training program you can start at any time. It's designed to be done on its own, without other strength or conditioning programs. The daily workouts can be completed in about 10 minutes, require NO EQUIPMENT, and can be done in a small indoor space.

This program combines martial arts and fitness to get you the exact workout you need on that day. It helps you build momentum to gain more out of your time – with your health, fitness, training, and the rest of your life.

These are just a sample of the programs we offer!

Looking to increase your speed? How about your fighting endurance? Visit whistlekick.com to see how we are revolutionizing the way you train to improve not only your martial arts skills, but also your overall health.

Check out the collection of whistlekick Programs in the whistlekick Store today!

We Truly Appreciate You!

Thank you for supporting whistlekick Books. We invite you to visit us at whistlekick.com. While there, you will find links to check out our other books, our store, social media, how to leave us reviews, info on our other projects, and much more.

We are always open to your thoughts, questions, and suggestions. You may contact us anytime at books@whistlekick.com.

Thank you!

wK Books